ARACHNID WORLD

TICKS

SANDRA MARKLE

LERNER PUBLICATIONS COMPANY MINNEAPOLIS

FOR CURIOUS KIDS EVERYWHERE

ACKNOWLEDGMENTS

The author would like to thank Dr. Thomas Mather, Tick Encounter Resource Center, University of Rhode Island, USA, and Dr. Simon Pollard, Canterbury Museum, Christchurch, New Zealand, for sharing their expertise and enthusiasm. A special thanks to Skip Jeffery for his support during the creation of this book.

Lerner Publications Company
A division of Lerner Publishing Group, Inc.
241 First Avenue North
Minneapolis, MN 55401 U.S.A.

Website address: www.lernerbooks.com

Library of Congress Cataloging-in-Publication Data

Markle, Sandra.
      Ticks : dangerous hitchhikers / by Sandra Markle.
          p.   cm. — (Arachnid world)
      Includes bibliographical references and index.
      ISBN 978-0-7613-5041-5 (lib. bdg. : alk. paper)
      1. Ticks—Juvenile literature. I. Title.
      QL458.15.P37M37 2011
      595.4′29—dc22   2010023484

Manufactured in the United States of America
1 - DP - 12/31/10

CONTENTS

AN ARACHNID'S WORLD

WELCOME TO THE WORLD OF ARACHNIDS

(ah-RACK-nidz). Arachnids can be found everywhere on Earth except in the deep ocean.

So how can you tell if an animal is an arachnid rather than a relative like the insect shown below? Both arachnids and insects belong to a group of animals called arthropods (AR-throh-podz). All the animals in this group share some traits. They have bodies divided into segments, jointed legs, and a stiff exoskeleton. This is a skeleton on the outside like a suit of armor. But one way to tell if an animal is an arachnid is to count its legs and main body parts. While not every adult arachnid has eight legs, most do. Arachnids have two main body parts. Adult insects have six legs and three main body parts. Some adult insects, like this mosquito *(right)*, also have wings. No arachnids have wings.

This book is about arachnids called ticks. Ticks are parasites. This means they live off other living things. Ticks, like this American dog tick, get the food they need by sucking another animal's blood. When ticks suck blood, they may also pass on diseases. In this way, ticks can make people and animals sick—even kill them. Ticks are little arachnids that cause big problems!

TICK FACT

A tick's
body temperature
rises and falls with the
temperature around it.
It must warm up to
be active.

OUTSIDE AND INSIDE

ON THE OUTSIDE

There are about nine hundred different types of ticks in the world. They all share certain features. One is having their two main body parts fused together. The front part of a tick's body is called the prosoma (PROH-soh-mah). The capitulum (ca-PIT-u-lum) looks like a tiny head, but it is really mouthparts. The tick's legs are attached to the prosoma. The back part of the tick's body is called the opisthosoma (oh-PIS-thoh-soh-mah). The tick's exoskeleton is made up of many hard plates connected by stretchy membrane. This lets the tick bend and move. It also lets the tick's body expand while feeding. Take a close look at the outside of a female deer tick to discover other key features.

LEGS: These are used for walking, climbing, and holding on. The legs are covered with short spines and end in a sharp-tipped claw.

OPISTHOSOMA

EYES:
A tick's eyes are located between the first and second legs. They probably can only tell light from dark.

HALLER'S ORGAN:
This sensory organ is in a pit near the end of the first pair of legs. It helps a tick smell when a host is nearby.

PALPS:
The palps stick out on either side of the mouthparts. The palps are covered with sensors that help the tick find a host's skin. The palps fold back against the host's skin when the tick inserts its hypostome. They cover and protect the hypostome when the tick is not feeding.

CAPITULUM

CHELICERAE
(KEH-liss-er-eye): This pair of small, clawlike parts has teeth along the edges to cut open a host's skin or covering.

HYPOSTOME
(heye-POH-stohm):
This needlelike part is below the chelicerae. Together they form a sucking tube. The hypostome stabs into the wound made by the chelicerae. Its backward-pointing teeth hold the tick to its host.

PROSOMA

ON THE INSIDE

Look at this drawing of the inside of an adult female tick.

TRACHEAE:
These tubes take in air through the spiracles. They send the oxygen in the air throughout the tick's body and release the waste gases.

BRAIN:
The brain receives messages from body parts and sends signals back to them.

PHARYNX (FAR-inks):
This muscular tube pumps food into the body's digestive system. Hairs in it filter out hard waste bits.

GONOPORE:
This is the female reproductive opening.

HEART:
This muscular tube pumps blood toward the head. The blood flows throughout the body and back to the heart.

MALPIGHIAN (mal-PIG-ee-an) TUBULES: This system of tubes cleans the blood of wastes and dumps them into the intestine.

OVARY:
This organ produces eggs.

NERVE GANGLIA:
These bundles of nerve tissue send messages between the brain and other body parts.

GUT:
Food is stored and digested here. The food passes into the tick's blood and is carried throughout the body.

SALIVARY GLAND:
This body part pours saliva (spit) and digestive juices into the wound site during a blood meal.

SPIRACLES:
These holes help ticks breathe by letting air into and out of the body.

Approved by
Dr. Thomas Mather,
Tick Encounter Resource Center,
University of Rhode Island

SOFT AND HARD TICKS

There are two main kinds of ticks—soft and hard. Check out some of the key differences between the two.

SOFT TICKS (LIKE THE RELAPSING FEVER TICK)

- They lack a shieldlike dorsal (back) plate. Their bodies are soft and leathery.
- Their mouthparts do not extend from their front end. They are most easily seen from below.
- The tick's saliva (spit) does not hold it to the host.
- Adults leave their host to mate.
- Males and females may feed and mate a number of times before dying. Females lay small batches of twenty to fifty eggs.

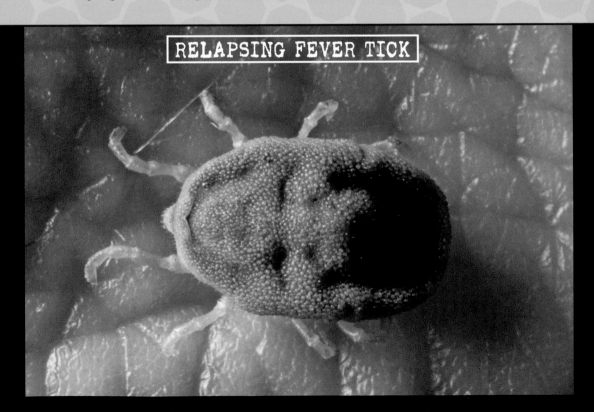

RELAPSING FEVER TICK

HARD TICKS (LIKE THE AMERICAN DOG TICK)

- The dorsal side of the opisthosoma is covered by a hard, shieldlike plate, called the scutum. The male's scutum covers its entire opisthosoma. The female's covers about one-third of it.
- The mouthparts extend forward from the head.
- The tick's saliva produces a kind of glue that holds the tick to the host while it feeds.
- Adults stay on their host when they mate.
- Males die after mating. The female dies after laying one batch of hundreds to thousands of eggs.

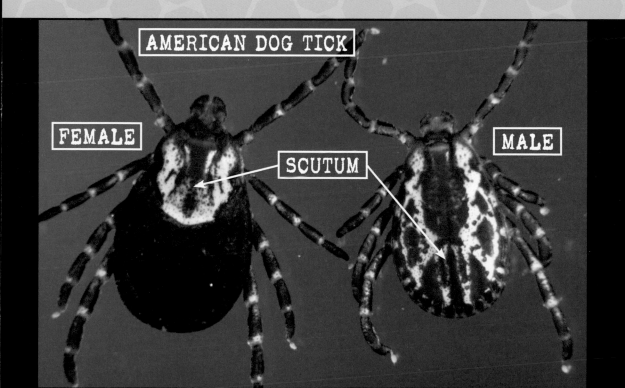

AMERICAN DOG TICK

FEMALE

SCUTUM

MALE

FEEDING TIME

Ticks feed on a host's blood. But they don't just poke their mouthparts into a blood vessel the way mosquitoes do. Their mouthparts are designed to snip open the host's skin or covering. This creates a shallow space and breaks open blood vessels. Blood pools in the space, and the tick sucks it in. As the tick feeds *(below)*, it also pours out some of its saliva. The saliva contains water, digestive juices, and special chemicals that keep the host's wound from healing. It may also contain microbes (tiny living things) such as bacteria that cause disease. The tick may have picked up these microbes during an earlier blood meal.

TICK FACT

Some of the chemicals in the tick's saliva numb the bite site. That way the host is less likely to feel a feeding tick and try to remove it.

Soft ticks, like relapsing fever ticks, usually take smaller meals than hard ticks. That's because their opisthosoma can't swell as much. Before a soft tick starts to feed, its opisthosoma looks wrinkled. As the tick eats, the wrinkles unfold. A soft tick can only swell as big as its unfolding skin allows. It is able to eat enough to increase its body weight about five to ten times.

Female hard ticks have a smaller hard plate or scutum on their back than males. So they can suck in more blood than a male. After feeding, the weight of a female dog tick will have increased nearly six hundred times.

TICK FACT

The hard scutum covering a male's back limits how much it can expand. So during a meal, males are usually only able to double their weight. In some kinds of ticks, the males don't eat at all.

SCUTUM

Look at all these layers of tissue. These make up the lower part of the scutum. They're the reason a hard tick can expand so much. Like a fan opening, these layers spread apart as the tick sucks in blood. As the tick feeds, the tough, flexible top layer of the scutum actually grows. The tick only sucks in a little blood during the first few days of its meal. This blood triggers the cells (the body's building blocks) of the top layer of the scutum to multiply. It quickly thickens. Then the tick finishes its meal in about a day, sucking in all the blood it can hold. The thickened covering stretches as the tissue layers fan out and the tick's opisthosoma balloons.

TICK FACT

A tick swells only at the end of its meal. So it is less likely to be noticed by the host or picked off before it has finished feeding.

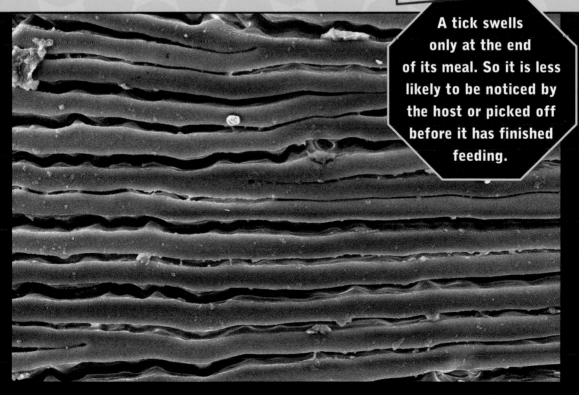

A tick may suck blood from more than one animal host during its lifetime. If one host is sick, a feeding tick may pick up microbes as it feeds. It may pass on the microbes to another host when it feeds again. The microbes remain in the tick's gut. When it starts feeding on a new host, the microbes feed on the blood pouring into the gut. They quickly multiply. Soon the many microbes spill out of the gut and circulate through the tick's body. Some end up in the salivary gland. As the tick feeds, it passes some of its saliva to the host. Then microbes in the salivary gland pour into the wound and go into the host's blood. They travel around the host's body.

While ticks spread other disease-causing microbes, these three have the greatest impact on people.

LYME DISEASE

symptoms: circular rash; flulike symptoms; and later, joint pain, nerve tingling, and trouble thinking clearly. This disease is treated with antibiotics (a medicine that kills disease-causing bacteria).

microbe: several kinds of *Borrelia* bacteria

tick carrier and location: a number of kinds of hard ticks, including sheep ticks and deer ticks *(right).* They are found in North America, Europe, and Asia.

ROCKY MOUNTAIN SPOTTED FEVER

symptoms: fever, muscle pains, flulike symptoms, and rash. This disease is treated with antibiotics.

microbe: *Rickettsia rickettsii* bacteria

tick carrier and location: American dog ticks and Rocky Mountain wood ticks *(right)* that live throughout the Americas

TICK-BORNE ENCEPHALITIS

symptoms: fever; flulike symptoms; and later, severe headache, trouble staying awake, confusion, and muscle spasms. A vaccine (something made from a weakened or killed disease-causing organism that's given to protect against a disease) is available. This disease can also be treated with special medicines that stop the virus from multiplying.

microbe: *Flavivirus* virus

tick carrier and location: a number of kinds of hard ticks, including sheep ticks *(right)* that live in Europe and Asia

BECOMING ADULTS

Like all arachnids, baby ticks become adults through incomplete metamorphosis. *Metamorphosis* means "change." A tick's life includes four stages: egg, larva, nymph, and adult. Except for having six legs instead of eight, tick larvae look like nymphs. Larvae and nymphs look and behave much like small adults. Larvae and nymphs are not able to reproduce.

SOME KINDS OF ARTHROPODS GO THROUGH COMPLETE METAMORPHOSIS. The four stages are egg, larva, pupa, and adult. Each stage looks and behaves very differently.

The nymph *(top right)* has seven legs instead of the usual eight. Most kinds of arachnids are able to regrow a lost part, like a leg, while they are still developing into adults. Ticks can't. If a part is lost, they must make do with the parts that remain.

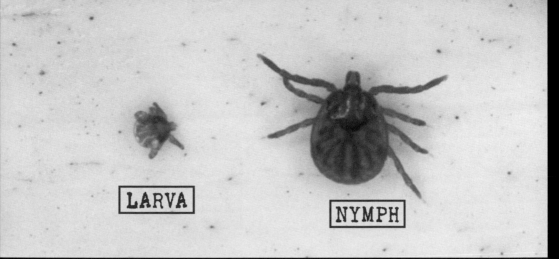

LARVA

NYMPH

LONE STAR TICK

ADULT FEMALE

19

LIFE CYCLE: ONE HOST

During each life stage, ticks need a blood meal to develop and grow big enough to molt, or shed their exoskeletons. Some kinds of hard ticks, such as cattle ticks, stay on the same host sucking its blood for their whole life. Only females ready to lay eggs drop off.

Life Cycle of a One-Host Tick (Cattle Tick)

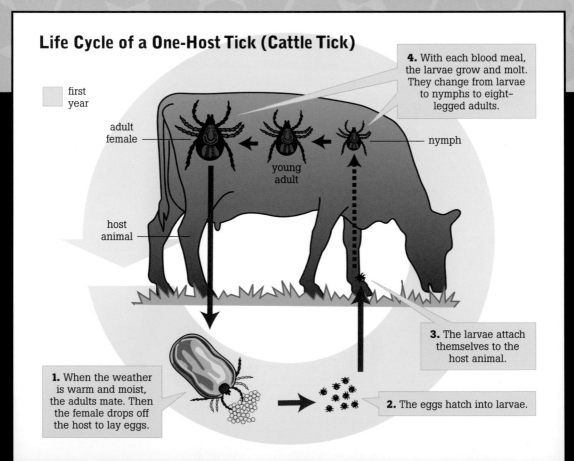

first year

4. With each blood meal, the larvae grow and molt. They change from larvae to nymphs to eight-legged adults.

adult female

young adult

nymph

host animal

3. The larvae attach themselves to the host animal.

1. When the weather is warm and moist, the adults mate. Then the female drops off the host to lay eggs.

2. The eggs hatch into larvae.

LIFE CYCLE: TWO HOSTS

Other kinds of hard ticks, like red-legged ticks, complete their life cycle on two hosts. The larvae hatch and feed on the first host. Then they drop off and spend the winter in a protected spot. In the spring, they become nymphs and attach to a second host. There they go through the nymph stage, become adults, and mate. The females drop off to deposit their eggs and restart the cycle.

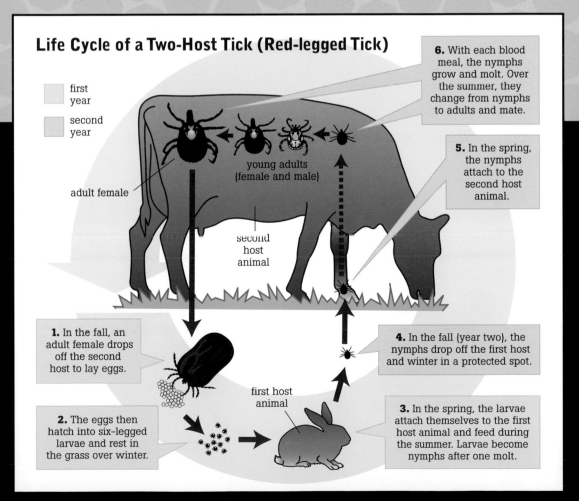

Life Cycle of a Two-Host Tick (Red-legged Tick)

first year

second year

adult female

young adults (female and male)

second host animal

6. With each blood meal, the nymphs grow and molt. Over the summer, they change from nymphs to adults and mate.

5. In the spring, the nymphs attach to the second host animal.

1. In the fall, an adult female drops off the second host to lay eggs.

2. The eggs then hatch into six-legged larvae and rest in the grass over winter.

first host animal

4. In the fall (year two), the nymphs drop off the first host and winter in a protected spot.

3. In the spring, the larvae attach themselves to the first host animal and feed during the summer. Larvae become nymphs after one molt.

LIFE CYCLE: THREE HOSTS

Soft ticks and most kinds of hard ticks, like the American dog tick, use three hosts to complete their life cycle. Eggs hatch on the ground in the fall and larvae rest in a sheltered spot during the winter. In the spring, the larvae attach to their first host. After feeding, they drop off the host and molt, becoming nymphs. Some nymphs find a new host right away. Others rest for a second winter and find a second host the following spring.

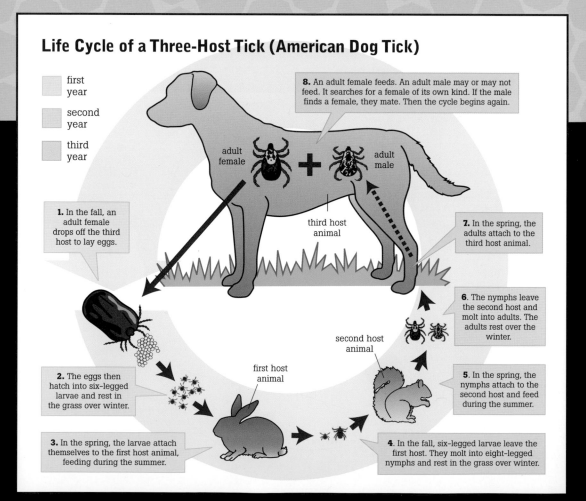

Life Cycle of a Three-Host Tick (American Dog Tick)

first year

second year

third year

8. An adult female feeds. An adult male may or may not feed. It searches for a female of its own kind. If the male finds a female, they mate. Then the cycle begins again.

adult female

adult male

1. In the fall, an adult female drops off the third host to lay eggs.

third host animal

7. In the spring, the adults attach to the third host animal.

6. The nymphs leave the second host and molt into adults. The adults rest over the winter.

second host animal

2. The eggs then hatch into six-legged larvae and rest in the grass over winter.

first host animal

5. In the spring, the nymphs attach to the second host and feed during the summer.

3. In the spring, the larvae attach themselves to the first host animal, feeding during the summer.

4. In the fall, six-legged larvae leave the first host. They molt into eight-legged nymphs and rest in the grass over winter.

After nymphs feed on the second host, they drop off and molt. This time they rest during the winter as adults. In the spring, they attach to a third host. After feeding, soft ticks drop off to mate. Most hard ticks mate on the host during the summer. Then the females drop off to deposit their eggs.

The timing of a tick's life cycle may vary depending on where it lives and the kind of tick it is.

TICK FACT

Unlike hard ticks, soft ticks go through several molts as larvae and as nymphs. They grow and change more slowly than hard ticks.

DOG TICK WAITING FOR HOST

A NEW BEGINNING

It is late May in England. Throughout the cool morning, a female sheep tick stays still, waiting. Over time, the sun's heat reaches her and warms her. She begins to crawl across the ground. She moves slowly. Her abdomen is swollen with eggs. These eggs have been forming inside her all winter long.

Finally, she stops and picks a spot in the leaf litter. There, one by one, she deposits nearly two thousand eggs. As each egg leaves her body, it merges with a sperm (a male reproductive cell). A baby tick starts to develop. A tough outer covering coats each egg. The female dies shortly after depositing her brood. Inside their eggs, the baby ticks grow and develop.

It's a warm day in late June when a female sheep tick larva *(below)* hatches. She stays hidden in the leaf litter. For one thing, it's damp there. Although ticks have a hard exoskeleton, their armor leaks. They tend to dry out quickly. To stay healthy, the female tick larva seeks a moist place to hide. It's also safer to hide among the bits of decaying leaves and alongside her thousands of brothers and sisters. Birds, beetles, ants, and spiders will eat any tick larvae they find.

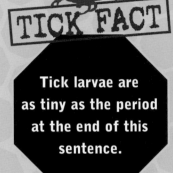

TICK FACT

Tick larvae are as tiny as the period at the end of this sentence.

BLOOD MEALS

FIRST BLOOD

Before the tick larva can grow bigger and continue to develop, she needs a blood meal. Special sensors on her front legs let her detect movement and heat. Other sensors detect the carbon dioxide gas animals give off when they breathe. When the female sheep tick larva senses all these things, she raises her front legs. A young rabbit brushes by the female tick larva and several of her siblings. The rabbit is a small host, but it's big enough to supply food for lots of tiny tick larvae. The female larva crawls through the rabbit's hair. Finally, she stops, grips the rabbit's skin, and snips open a tiny slit. She pushes her mouthparts into this wound and feeds.

MEAL TWO PLUS MICROBES

With her abdomen swollen from her blood meal, the female sheep tick larva drops off her host. She crawls into damp leaf litter and stays safely hidden for nearly a year. All that time, she lives off her first blood meal.

By the time spring comes again, she's grown too big for her exoskeleton and molts. Her new bigger body has four pairs of legs instead of just three pairs. She's now a nymph. Once her new exoskeleton hardens, she crawls up to the surface of the leaf litter and climbs onto a plant. Day after day, she waits for a host. Sometimes, when her body becomes dry, she climbs down into the leaf litter. There she soaks up moisture. Then she climbs up again to continue waiting. Some nymphs never find a host and they die. But this female tick nymph senses a host is close. She stretches out her two front legs.

TICK FACT

Lone star ticks don't stay in one place to wait for a host. They crawl, sometimes more than 30 feet (about 10 meters), in search of a meal.

When a dog walks past, the female sheep tick nymph grabs onto the dog's hair with her claw-tipped legs. Then she climbs up the dog's body. Ticks often feed near an animal's ears or eyes because blood vessels are close to the surface in those areas. The female tick nymph settles between the dog's eyes.

She feeds until she's full. This time, though, her meal includes more than blood. The blood she sucks in has *Borrelia burgdorferi* bacteria in it. The dog has Lyme disease. Its owner thought his pet was being lazy, but the animal has a fever and achy joints. About three weeks earlier, the dog was bitten by a different tick. That tick infected it with the bacteria.

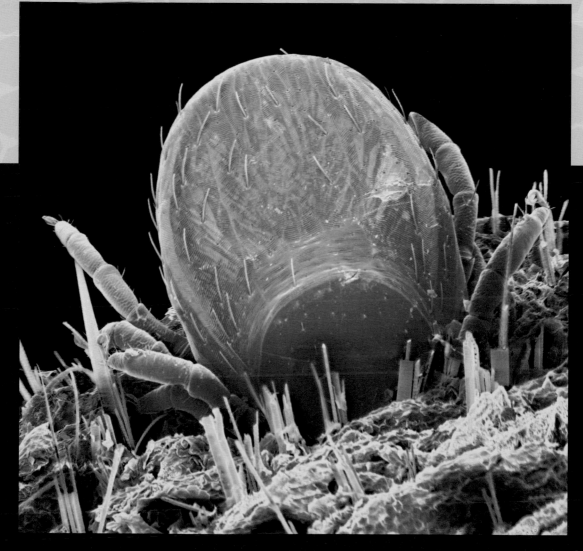

After she fed on the dog's blood, the tick nymph has the worm-shaped bacteria *(below)* in her gut. They pass through the walls of the nymph's stomach and are carried by the blood throughout her body. The bacteria don't seem to affect the nymph. As her blood meal is digested, the bacteria settle in her empty gut. The tick nymph drops off her host.

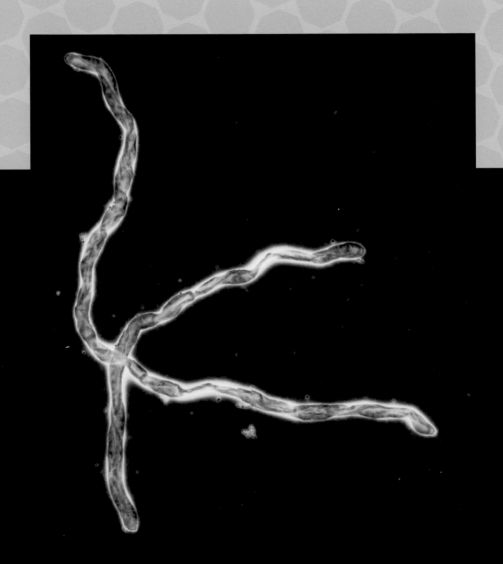

MEAL THREE WITH A MATE

When fall arrives again, the female sheep tick nymph molts once more and becomes an adult. Then the young adult female finds a place in the leaf litter and rests through the winter. In the spring, she is ready for another meal and to reproduce.

A little over a month passes before a little boy and his mother brush past. The female sheep tick grabs onto the woman's pant leg and starts to climb. The tick is so tiny the woman doesn't notice it crawling under her shirt and up her back. Back home, the woman checks her son's body for ticks. She checks herself too, but she doesn't find the tiny tick on her neck.

The female sheep tick starts her third and final meal. As she sucks in blood, the *Borrelia* bacteria in her stomach begin to feed too. A day later, the bacteria begin reproducing. Soon there are lots more *Borrelia* bacteria. Many pass through the walls of the tick's gut and into its blood. Some travel to the salivary gland. As the female tick feeds, she pours saliva and *Borrelia* bacteria into the tiny wound she made. On the third day of the tick's meal, the woman feels a lump on her neck. She looks in the mirror and spots the tick. It has swollen large enough for her to see it. She calls her husband. He uses tweezers and carefully removes the tick and flushes it down the toilet.

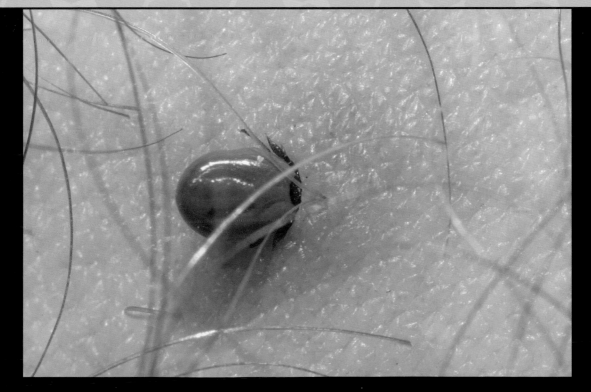

About two weeks later, the woman starts having headaches. Her arms and legs ache. She develops a target–shaped rash where the tick was attached. She knows these are early symptoms of Lyme disease, so she goes to her doctor. A blood test shows she has Lyme disease.

TICK FACT

In the United States, more than twenty thousand people each year get Lyme disease as a result of tick bites.

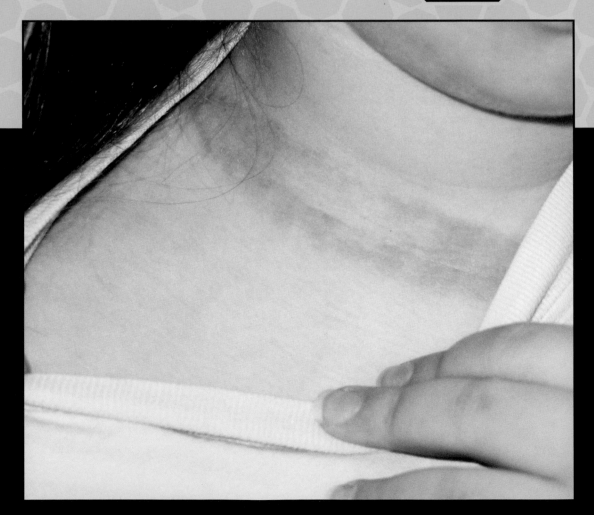

If the woman had left her symptoms untreated, she could have developed severe joint pain and numbness in her hands and feet. The doctor gives her an antibiotic. Within a few weeks, she is fine again. She's also learned an important lesson. The best protection against tick bites is to prevent ticks from getting onto the body in the first place. From then on, she is even more careful to protect herself and her family from ticks. She looks for new lines of clothing *(below)* that have been made to protect against ticks and other insects.

THE CYCLE CONTINUES

Being plucked off its host was the end of one female sheep tick's life cycle. Other adult female sheep ticks latch onto animals, such as dogs passing through the grass or sheep in a pasture. While these adult females are feeding, they give off special chemicals, called pheromones. Like perfume, the chemicals spread in the air. Ticks can only mate with other ticks of their own kind. Any male sheep ticks sharing a female's host quickly start tracking her pheromones.

SHEEP TICK ATTACHED TO A DOG

Male sheep ticks don't even waste time feeding. The adult male's mouthparts don't work well. They feed only a little, if at all, on this third host. They are on the host to find a mate. If a male sheep tick finds a female sheep tick, he crawls under her while she's still feeding. He inserts his sperm into her gonopore. Shortly after mating, the male tick drops off the host and dies. The female finishes her meal. Then she too drops off. It's time for her to rest for the winter while her eggs mature.

In the spring, before she dies, the adult female sheep tick deposits her nearly two thousand eggs. The tick larvae develop inside their eggs. The tick's cycle of life continues.

BELLY SIDE OF FEMALE

PREVENT TICK BITES

Because a tick's bite can make you sick, follow these tips to protect yourself and your family from ticks.

When you're going outdoors, especially in areas with lots of plants or tall grass, dress smartly. Wear socks, a long-sleeved shirt or jacket, and long pants. Secure cuffs tightly at wrists and ankles.

Spray the clothes you wear outdoors with an insect repellent containing a chemical called permethrin.

Larvae and nymphs are often in leaf litter. Avoid sitting on the ground in leaf litter.

TICK FACT

Some animals protect other animals from ticks. This red deer is being checked for ticks by a jackdaw. The bird tugs out and gulps down any ticks it finds. This helps both the bird and the deer.

When you return home, check your body for ticks. Have someone else check your hair and the back of your neck and ears.

If a tick is embedded in your skin, remove it using tweezers *(below)*. Grab the tick where the mouthparts pierce the skin. Tug gently but firmly. Immediately treat the wound with antiseptic. Contact your doctor to check if you need to take an antibiotic.

TICK FACT

Female Rocky Mountain wood ticks can pass on *Rickettsia* bacteria to their eggs. This causes Rocky Mountain spotted fever. The young hatch, ready to spread these disease-causing microbes to their hosts.

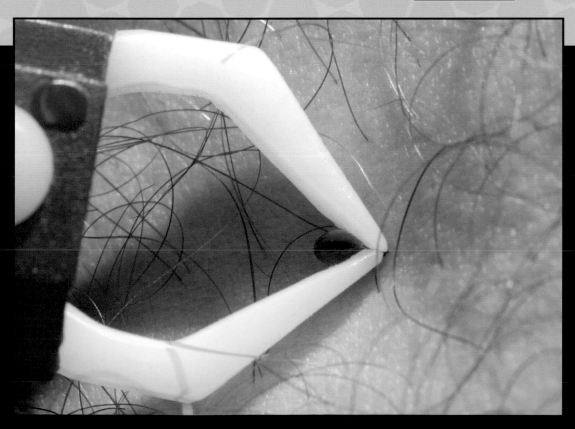

TICKS AND OTHER ARACHNID TROUBLEMAKERS

Ticks belong to a group, or order, of arachnids called Ixodida (ick–ZAH–di–duh). There are about nine hundred different kinds of ticks—hard and soft. All are parasites. They feed on blood they suck from other living animals. Scientists group living and extinct animals with others that are similar. So ticks are classified this way:

kingdom: Animalia
phylum: Arthropoda
class: Arachnida
order: Ixodida

HELPFUL OR HARMFUL? Ticks are both, but they are mainly harmful. They're helpful because they provide food for other animals, such as birds. But they harm people and animals by spreading disease-causing microbes. The most common disease spread by ticks in North America is Lyme disease.

HOW BIG IS an adult sheep tick? A female is 0.09 inch (2.5 mm) long. That's only a little bigger than a sesame seed. An adult male is slightly smaller.

MORE ARACHNID TROUBLEMAKERS

Compare the problems ticks cause to the trouble created by these arachnids.

MAGNIFIED VIEW

***Varroa* mites**, especially a kind called *Varroa destructor*, attack honeybees. Each mite attaches itself to the body of either a bee adult or larva. It pierces the bee's body and sucks its fluids. This may weaken the bee so much it dies. The mite may also pass on viruses. One virus deforms an adult bee's wings so it can't fly. This mite is causing great problems in bee colonies. It affects honey production and harms plants that the bees usually pollinate (spread pollen from plant to plant as part of the plant's life cycle).

Arizona bark scorpions are common in the southwestern United States. They're little, only about 3 inches (7 centimeters) long. These little scorpions frequently slip into people's homes and garages. There, they may go unnoticed until someone accidentally touches them or steps on them. Bark scorpions defend themselves by delivering a dose of venom with a flick of their stinger-tipped tail. They are the most venomous scorpion in North America. Their sting can cause intense pain that lasts for hours. It can be deadly for a young child, someone who is already unwell, or someone who suffers an allergic reaction.

MAGNIFIED VIEW

Two-spotted spider mites are only 0.015 inches (0.4 mm) long, but they're big troublemakers for two reasons. They damage plants by poking their mouthparts into plant cells to feed. And they grow and reproduce superfast. A female two-spotted spider mite can produce eggs just five days after hatching. She will lay an average of five eggs a day for about a month. These mites cluster together with others in a colony that can destroy plant crops. They'll attack more than one hundred different kinds of plants both outdoors and in greenhouses.

GLOSSARY

adult: the final stage of an arachnid's life cycle. They are able to reproduce at this stage.

brain: the organ that receives messages from body parts and sends signals to control them

capitulum: the part of a tick that has the mouthparts and the palps

chelicerae: a pair of small clawlike parts near the mouth. These are edged with teeth to cut open the host's skin or covering. They form the upper half of the tick's sucking mouthparts.

egg: a female reproductive cell; also the name given to the first stage of an arachnid's life cycle

exoskeleton: the protective, armorlike covering on the outside of an arachnid's body

eyes: the sensory organs that detect light and send signals to the brain for sight. Ticks's eyes are located between the first and second pairs of legs, but not all ticks have eyes.

gonopore: the female reproductive opening

gut: the place where food is stored and digested before passing into the tick's blood

Haller's organ: the sensory organ in a pit near the foot end of the first pair of legs. This organ is unique to ticks. It helps a tick smell when a host is nearby.

heart: the muscular tube that pumps blood throughout the body

hypostome: a needlelike part below the chelicerae that forms half of the tick's sucking tube. It usually has backward-pointing teeth to hold the tick to the host.

larva: the first immature, six-legged stage of a tick's life

legs: the limbs used for walking, climbing, and hanging onto a host

Malpighian tubules: a system of tubes that cleans the blood of wastes and dumps them into the intestine

microbes: microscopic living things, such as disease-causing bacteria

molt: the process of an arachnid shedding its exoskeleton

nerve ganglia: bundles of nerve tissue that send messages between the brain and other body parts

nymph: the second immature stage of the tick's life cycle. The nymph has eight legs and looks and behaves much like an adult. However, it is smaller and unable to reproduce.

opisthosoma: the back part of a tick's body

organisms: living plants or animals

ovary: the body part that produces eggs

palps: a part on either side of the mouthparts. The palps are covered with sensors that let the tick home in on a host's skin. They cover and protect the hypostome when it is not feeding.

pharynx: a muscular body part that contracts to create a pumping force, drawing food into the body's digestive system

pheromones: chemical scents given off as a form of communication

prosoma: the front part of a tick's body. It includes the capitulum and the legs.

salivary gland: an organ that produces saliva. During a blood meal, this gland pours saliva plus water and digestive juices into the wound site. Disease organisms, if present, migrate to this gland and are then transferred to the host.

scutum: the shieldlike plate on the back of hard ticks

sperm: a male reproductive cell

spiracles: openings that let air enter and exit the tracheae

tracheae: tubes that carry oxygen throughout the tick's body

DIGGING DEEPER

To keep on investigating ticks, explore these books and online sites.

BOOKS

Fredericks, Anthony D. *Bloodsucking Creatures.* New York: Franklin
Watts, 2003. Compare ticks to other bloodsucking animals.

Silverstein, Alvin, Virginia Silverstein, and Laura Silverstein Nunn.
Lyme Disease. Danbury, CT: Children's Press, 2000. Investigate the
symptoms, treatment, and prevention of this disease spread by ticks.

Townsend, John. *Incredible Arachnids.* Chicago: Heinemann-Raintree,
2005. See how ticks are like other arachnids and how they're different.

WEBSITES

CDC Features: Stop Ticks
http://www.cdc.gov/Features/StopTicks/
Discover ways to protect yourself and your
pets from ticks. Follow links to learn more
about diseases people can get from a tick.

Life Cycle of Babesia microti
http://www.youtube.com/
watch?v=J0akxoorjoQ
Real video and animation combine for a close-up look at a tick's life
cycle. Also find out about one of the blood-disease-causing organisms
ticks spread when they bite.

University of Rhode Island's Tick Encounter Resource Center:
Think Tick . . . Take Action!
http://www.tickencounter.org/
This site is packed with information, videos, and pictures. Don't miss the
how-to videos for removing ticks. Go to the "Interact" section to have fun
learning about ticks and avoiding tick bites.

LERNER SOURCE

Visit
for free, downloadable arachnid
diagrams, research assignments
to use with this series, and
additional information about
arachnid scientific names.

TICK ACTIVITY

Follow these steps to see firsthand how ticks spread disease-causing organisms.

1. Pour water into two clear glasses. To one glass, add one teaspoonful of rainbow-colored nonpareils (cookie and candy sprinkles available in the bakery section of grocery stores).

2. Wait a few seconds for the nonpareils to sink to the bottom. Poke a plastic straw straight down into the candy bits. Cover the top of the straw with the tip of your index finger and lift. When you stop air from rushing down into the straw, you trap whatever liquid is inside the straw.

3. Place the straw in the glass of clean water. Take your finger off the top of the straw and lift it out of the water. Look closely. You should see that a few of the nonpareils have been moved to the clean water. If not, repeat until you do.

This is the way ticks spread microbes from host to host. Microbes usually multiply so quickly it only takes a few to start disease-causing symptoms.

MORE FROM SANDRA MARKLE

INSECT WORLD:
Diving Beetles
Hornets
Locusts
Luna Moths
Mosquitoes
Praying Mantises
Stick Insects
Termites

INDEX

PHOTO ACKNOWLEDGMENTS

The images in this book are used with the permission of: © Dwight Kuhn, pp. 4, 5; The University of Rhode Island Tick Encounter Resource Center, pp. 6-7; © Eye of Science/Photo Researchers, Inc., pp. 7 (both insets), 12, 32; © Dr. James L. Castner/Visuals Unlimited, Inc., pp. 10, 19; © Dr. Robert Calentine/Visuals Unlimited, Inc., pp. 11, 16; © O.S.F./Animals Animals, p. 13; © David Wrobel/Visuals Unlimited, Inc., p. 14; © Electron Microscopy Unit, Cancer Research UK/Anne Weston/Visuals Unlimited, Inc., p. 15; © Science Source/Photo Researchers, Inc., p. 17 (top); © Jan Van Der Knokke/Minden Pictures, p. 17 (bottom); © Darlyne A. Murawski/National Geographic/Getty Images, p. 23; © Kim Taylor/Minden Pictures, pp. 24-25, 30; © Wim van Egmond/Visuals Unlimited, Inc., pp. 26, 33; © Gary Carter/Visuals Unlimited, Inc., p. 27; © London Scientific Films/Oxford Scientific/Photolibrary, pp. 28-29; © Volker Steger/Photo Researchers, Inc., pp. 31, 39; © MStolt/Photolibrary, p. 34 (left); © Kurt Friedrich Möbus/imagebroker.net/Photolibrary, p. 34 (right); © Solvin Zankl/Visuals Unlimited, Inc., pp. 35, 41; © Arthur Glauberman/Photo Researchers, Inc., p. 36; © Stephen Chernin/Getty Images, p. 37; © Kim Taylor/naturepl.com, p. 38; © David Tipling/Oxford Scientific/Photolibrary, p. 40; © Dr. Dennis Kunkel/Visuals Unlimited, Inc., p. 43 (top); © Doug Sokell/Visuals Unlimited, Inc., p. 43 (middle); © Nigel Cattlin/Visuals Unlimited, Inc., p. 43 (bottom). Illustrations by © Bill Hauser/Independent Picture Service, pp. 8-9; © Laura Westlund/Independent Picture Service, pp. 20, 21, 22.

Front cover: Centers for Disease Control and Prevention Public Health Image Library/James Gathany.